Seven Sacred Circles

The Order of Encircling from *Sefer Maavar Yabbok*

שבעה מעגלי קדש

ספר מעבר יבק – סדר ההקפות

Rabbi T'mimah Audrey Ickovits

Print Layout: Hamotzi Press http://www.hamotzipress.com

ISBN: 9798829350468

Cover Picture: "The Seven Circuits," Bernard Picart (1673-1733),
© Royal Library of the Hague

Imprint: Independently published by Holistic Jew

© 2022 Rabbi T'mimah Audrey Ickovits
www.HolisticJew.org
RabbiTmimah@HolisticJew.org
151 Ocean Park Boulevard
Santa Monica, CA 90405

Gustave Doré, ***Jacob Wrestling with the Angel****, 1855. Engraving on paper.*

TABLE OF CONTENTS

Appreciation and Acknowledgment 6

Introduction 7

About Sefer Maavar Yabbok 8

The Secret of Seven 11

Hakafot - Encircling 13

Combining Hakafot with Seven 15

About Ana B'khoaḥ 16

Orchestrating Seder Ha-Hakafot 18

When is Seder Ha-Hakafot Done 19

Matbe'a (Structure) Of Seder Ha-Hakafot 20

Seder Ha-Hakafot for Women 22

Seder Ha-Hakafot for Men 34

Probing the Mystery 46

About the Translator 57

Appreciation and Acknowledgment

Deep Gratitude

David Zinner, Founding and Past Executive Director, Kavod v'Nichum

Rabbi Oren Z. Steinitz, PhD

Eshet Hayyil Emunah Fialkoff

Rena Boroditsky, Gamliel Institute

Rabbi Joe Blair, Gamliel Institute

Special Thanks

Daniel C. Matt, PhD

for consulting on this work

Appreciation

Ya'qub Ibn Yusuf
Kerry Swartz, Gamliel Institute
Rabbi Janet Madden, PhD
Rick Light, Gamliel Institute
Rabbi Ivan Ickovits

Introduction

Many fond memories are made by encircling in Jewish tradition – beneath a *ḥuppah* (wedding canopy) during wedding rituals, around a Torah with a *lulav* and *etrog* on *Sukkot*, dancing with a Torah on *Simḥat Torah*, or simply being in community while such rituals are happening. Each of these are joyful moments in Jewish life.

Just as encircling accompanies some of the most important events of our Jewish lives, so too it is used to honor departure from life. This book, *Seven Sacred Circles*, seeks to make the *Seder Ha-Hakafot* (the order of encircling) accessible to those performing the sacred mitzvah of tending to the dead. It represents a meaningful and potent final act of honor to the departed.

This ancient ritual is taken from the first and most respected traditional Hebrew book on end-of-life care –*Sefer Maavar Yabok*– authored by Rabbi Aharon Berekhiah *z"l* in 1626. In it, he attributes this ritual of seven *hakafot* around a *nifteret/niftar* (deceased) to *Hillel ha-zaken* (Hillel the Elder).[1]

This book includes two versions of Hebrew text—one adapted for use by women as well as the original text written for men. In addition, the book includes English translation and transliteration for both versions.

Seven Sacred Circles begins by drawing from Kabbalah with a step-by-step explanation of the structure behind the ritual. First, the number seven is contextualized from both secular and Jewish perspectives. Then, a light is shined on *hakafot* – sacred encircling with intentions for each orbit. Next, the structure and movement of the seven circles are illuminated through a sacred poem. Finally, the powerful liturgy for seven *hakafot*, the *Seder Ha-Hakafot*, is presented.

Though this book focuses on *hakafot* around the deceased, the structure outlined here is useful every time a ritual of seven, *hakafot*, or seven *hakafot* is done. The methodology is therefore applicable beyond this particular ritual.

Encircling offers a physical means of expressing emotion during times of celebration as well as times of mourning. If you are a ritualist, prayer leader, officiate life cycle events, provide care for those dying, or you are in love with Kabbalah, this book is for you.

Orchestration of Seder Ha-Hakafot can be found on page 18, liturgy for women begins on page 22, and liturgy for men begins on page 34.

About Sefer Maavar Yabbok

Sefer Maavar Yabbok is a window into Jewish culture and community in the 17th century. It was written by the Master of Kabbalah, Rabbi Aharon Berekhiah of Modena, Italy and published in Mantua, Italy in 1626 CE. It provides a series of rituals, practices, and methods to support people nearing the end of life. It includes guidance for caring for the sick, bedside presence, the moment of death, and how to provide care after the transition. Additionally, it is a portal into subtle ways to move energy taught through the language of Kabbalah.

The term "*Maavar Yabbok*" refers to Yaakov Avinu's[1] crossing the River Yabbok. Yaakov tenaciously overpowers an angel. He receives the name Yisra'el[2] to recognize his enlightenment. Just as Yaakov crossed over into another realm to discover his own higher being, the *meitah* or *meit* is preparing to cross over into a new reality.

ספר
מעבר יבק
ווילנא

The image on the right is the cover page of *Sefer Maavar Yabbok*. It references the 1895 Vilna edition.

The image on the left is the liturgy of the practice being explored in this book – *Seder Ha-Hakafot* (The Order of Encircling). Jewish liturgy has typically been written in the masculine. The Hebrew in this image is the Hebrew for use by men that appears in this book.

1 Our Ancestor Yaakov, a.k.a. Jacob son of Isaac, as described in Genesis 32:23.

2 **יִשְׂרָאֵל** Yisrael 1) The lineage of Yisrael, Yaakov, 2) parsing the Hebrew word gives **יָשָׁר אֵל** *Yashar Eyl*, Direct to *Eyl* (G!D), 3) Permuting the letters offers שִׁיר אֵל *Shir Eyl* - Song of *Eyl* (G!D) 4) G!D-Wrestlers 5) Parsing the letters offers יש רא״ל *Yesh Ra-el*, literally "there are 231" referencing the 231 gates of creation that are derived from the distinct 2-letter combinations of the 22 letters of the Aleph Bet - from which creation manifested. *Sefer Yetzirah* 2:4 ר א ל is 200+30+1 = 231 in gematria.

A Continuum of End-of-Life Care

Sefer Maavar Yabbok is written for the members of the *ḥevrah kadisha* (Sacred Society) to deepen their understanding and practice of holistic end-of-life care and provide honor to the dead and comfort to the mourners. It is a comprehensive collection of commentary, practice, and liturgy supporting needs at the end of life, couched in wisdom of classical Kabbalah. It incorporates a range of tools to support the *neshamah* (soul), mourners, community, and the *ḥevrah* members.

It calls for community to be at the bedside with those who are ill—praying for them and with them, reciting Psalms, and learning Torah—in addition to providing a step-by-step ritual to honor the deceased through loving and sacred preparation of the body for burial following death.

The key periods of end-of-life care addressed in *Sefer Maavar Yabbok* include:

1. *Bikur Ḥolim*, visiting the sick
2. *Eyt Yetziat HaNeshamah*, the time (period) the soul leaves
3. *Sh'mirah*, guarding the body
4. *Tohorah*, caring for the dead
5. *L'vaya*, accompanying the body for burial

Maavar Yabbok teaches a full continuum of care for these stages. It includes 112 verses offered for visiting the sick.[3] As the soul prepares to transition, it offers a practice for *vidui* (confession) and prayers to support the *neshamah* (soul) in transition. Then, following death, it shares practices and rituals for washing, *tohorah* (ritual pouring or *mikveh*), dressing, funeral, burial, and ways of comforting mourners.

In this way, the *ḥevrah* offers help to the living through the *mitzvah* of *bikkur holim*, visiting the unwell. *Sefer Maavar Yabbok* confirms that having (well behaved) loved ones present at the moment of death brings great pleasure to

---

3 112 is the gematria for *Yabbok* (יבק) as in *Maavar Yabbok* (מעבר יבק) (10 = י, 2 = ב, 100 = ק) 10+2+100=112. 112 is the summation of the gematria of three Divine Names on the center axis of the Tree of Life *Ehyeh* (*Keter*) 21, YHVH (*Tiferet*) 26, and Adonai (*Sh'khinah/Malkhut*) 65. The 112 verses model movement through the center line of the Tree of Life offering blessing for a safe, sacred, and unburdened transition from life to death.

the dying. It is a powerful and good omen (*Segulah*) to depart while hearing sacred songs. When someone does die, focus naturally remains on tending to the needs of the newly deceased.

The practice of sitting with the dead prior to burial is called *sh'mirah*, guarding. The gentle transition of presence from *bikkur ḥolim* to *sh'mirah* offers honor to the deceased.

The practices today in many *ḥevrot k'doshot* (plural for *ḥevrah kadisha*) differ considerably from what is written in *Maavar Yabbok*. Liturgy changes for a variety of reasons – customs mingle, needs change, resources vary, educational levels differ, etc.

Seven Sacred Circles brings forward one of the most interesting parts of *Sefer Maavar Yabbok* – the practice of *hakafot* (encircling) around the *meitah* or *meit*. *Hakafot* are done following *tohorah* and casketing, but before burial. *Hakafot* can be done near the *tohorah* room in a chapel or synagogue, by the *ḥevrah kadisha* or by the whole community. Through this uplifting ritual, the *meit* or *meitah* is escorted into the next cycle with movement and blessing.

Traditional liturgy and commentary have been developed by men, for men. This document seeks to provide balance by introducing Hebrew adapted for use for women.

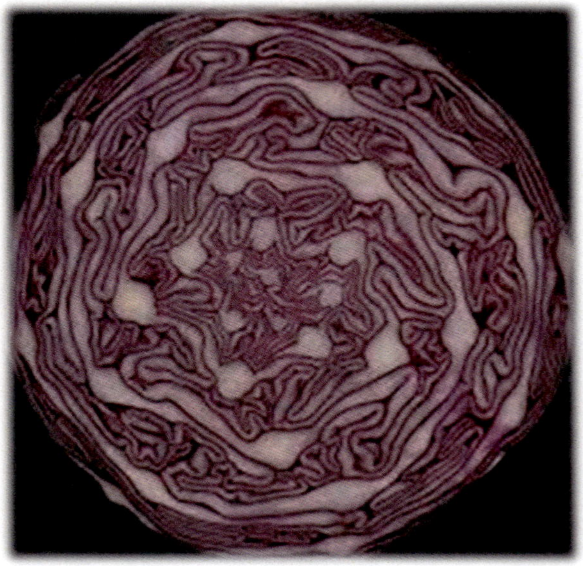

Purple cabbage: circles within circles reoccur in nature.

The Secret of Seven

Before we dive into the *Seder Ha-Hakafot*, let us explore some of the ways seven and encircling resonate with both our physical and spiritual existence.

Seven represents a spiritual energy that holds our world together. It is a number signaling completion in the physical world. Torah teaches that the world was created in six primordial days, *"Yamim"*. On the seventh primordial day, The Creator paused and ensouled the world (*shavat vayinafash*).

A perfect circle can be surrounded by exactly six circles of the same size. The center circle, then, is the unifying and vitalizing force of the other six. Similarly, Shabbat is the vitalizing force for the other six days of the week. So too, the spiritual realm, represented by the number seven, acts as a centering and vivifying force for the power of six, which represents the physical world. This can be seen in the six directions of our space-time continuum.

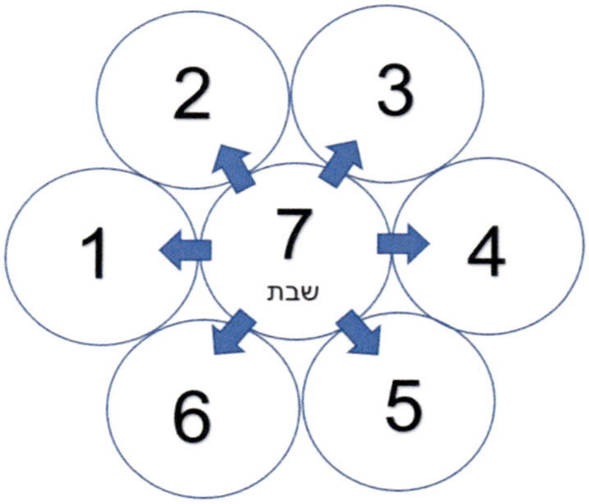

Seven as the central power that energizes the physical domain of six.

The word for seven in Hebrew is *"sheva"*. Interestingly, in a different context the same root translates as oath. In yet another context the word translates as contentment. There is a deep resonance of this root word, which delivers an important message. When one takes on the **oath** of **seven** (as in the observance of Shabbat), thereby cultivating spiritual energy in the physical world, **contentment** follows.

The Shabbat liturgy affirms that *Yisrael* is an "*Am Mekadshei Sh'vi'i*" – a people who bring forward the holiness of seven.[4] Wherever seven appears in a spiritual practice, the Secret of Seven can be used to deepen the experience. See "Probing the Mystery," on page 46 for more detail.

---

[4] See, for example, the fourth blessing of the Shabbat *Musaf Amidah* in Ashkenazi liturgy.

EXAMPLES OF SEVEN

Seven is the number of completion within the natural world. Notice how prevalent this number is in nature and in Torah.

- **SECULAR**
  - Seven days of the week
  - Seven colors of the rainbow
  - Seven wonders of the world
  - Seven continents
  - Seven natural notes on western musical scale
  - Seven openings in the head: two eyes, two ears, two nostrils, one mouth
- **BIBLICAL AND RABBINIC**
  - Seven days of creation
  - Seven ancestors - three patriarchs plus four matriarchs
  - Seven candles in a *menorah*
  - Seven prongs on the two shins of *t'fillin:* one has three and the other has four
  - Seven years of bounty and seven years of famine in Yoseph's dream
  - Seven days of Passover and *Sukkot* according to Torah
  - Seven drops of blood for the Temple sacrifice ritual
  - Seven years of *Sh'mitah* cycle
  - Seven *Sh'mitah* cycles for the Jubilee
  - Seven weeks of seven days counting the *omer*
  - Seven Hebrew double letters - *Bet, Gimel, Dalet, Kaf, Peh, Resh, Tav*
  - Seven heavens
  - Seven lower *S'firot*
  - Seven lines in the *Ana B'khoaḥ* (see page 17)
- **DEATH AND MOURNING**
  - Seven-day purification ritual (in Torah) for those who touched a dead body
  - Seven stops to a gravesite before burial
  - Seven days of *Shiva*

Hakafot - Encircling

Encircling is a foundational pattern of existence on Earth.

A Circle is Non-Hierarchical

The first thing we notice about a circle is its egalitarian shape. It has no hierarchy—every point on a circle is equidistant from the center. Likewise, it has no end and no beginning, no head, and no tail.

The Holy Rebbe Tzvi Elimelekh of Dinov, author of the B'nay Yisaskhar[5], teaches the meaning of the circular dance of the Tzaddikim in The World that is Coming.[6] He explains that in a circular dance, everyone gets their moment to shine just as each of the constellations of the zodiac shines during its designated time period. There is no jealousy, only appreciation and acceptance.

Encircling Stimulates Life

An elemental form of encircling that impacts us daily is the orbiting of the planets. As we know, just as the power of seven serves as a focal point for the six dimensions of the space-time continuum, so too a planet or star acts as a focal point, attracting objects around it into orbit through its gravitational pull. We see then that orbiting is an act of responding to the pull of a central force.

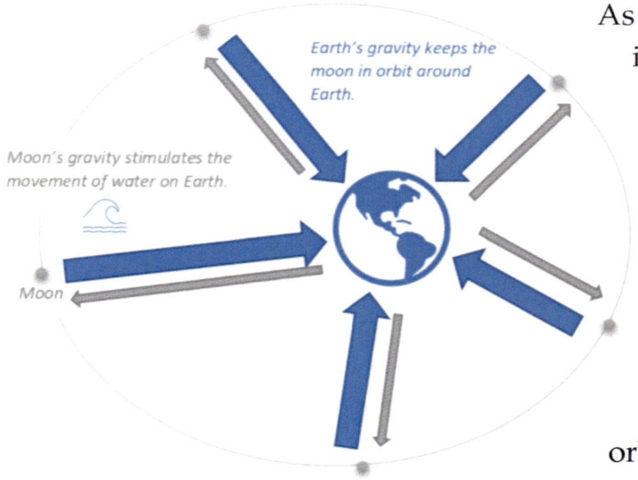

As Moon orbits Earth, its mass exerts its own gravitational pull. This initiates ongoing movement on Earth by creating waves in large bodies of water.

Life *is* movement.[7] Thus – just as a central force acts to stimulate orbits around itself, so too those orbits act to give life to the central force. In other words, orbital movements stimulate life.

---

[5] Adapted from *B'nay Yisaskhar Maamrey Tammuz-Av Mamar Daled* aleph-bet (4:1-2)

[6] *Bavli Ta'anit 26b*

[7] *Life on Land* by Emilie Conrad, 2007

Beyond its importance for initiating movement, the tension between celestial entities creates the cosmic glue that allows the solar system and beyond to be stable. These fragile, yet balanced orbits keep our universe in check.

Additionally, orbits define our entire experience of space and time on Earth. What is a day other than Earth's full turn on her axis every 23 hours, 56 minutes and 4.1 seconds? What is a year other than Earth's completed orbit around the Sun every 365.256 days? These movements define Earth's unique space-time continuum—days, months, and years.

Thus, a series of orbital or encircling movements make up the foundation of our experience—initiating movement on our planet, stabilizing our universe, and defining our experience of time and space.

It is important to note that a perfect circle does not exist in nature. This is due to the pull of gravity among celestial bodies, which distorts circular motion.

Encircling is intrinsic to life as we know it.

It is no wonder that *hakafot* (circle dances) are notably present in Jewish ritual.

- Torah Service - circuit around community with Torah before and after reading.
- *Tu B'Av* – "*B'toolot B'maḥol*" maidens dance in a circle on the full moon of the month of Av to meet their beloved.
- *Tzaddikim* dancing in a circle in *Olam HaBa* – The World that is Coming.
- Israeli folk dancing (*rikudei 'am*) is often done in a circle.

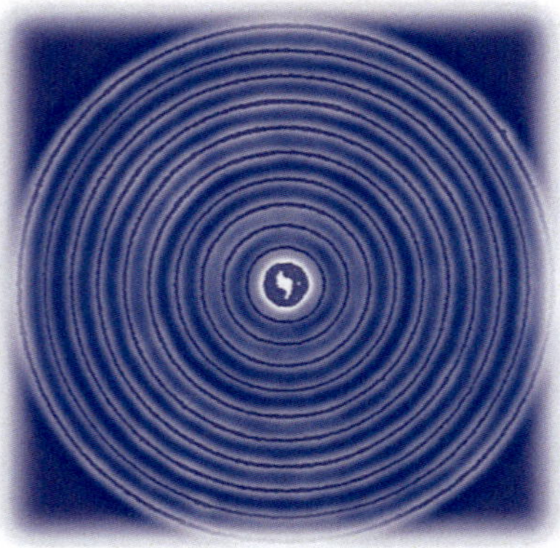

"Feminine Tree of Life" commentary attributed to Rivaad on Sefer Yetzirah 1:2 Jerusalem 5767

Combining Hakafot with Seven

Combining encircling (*hakafot*) with the number seven is extremely powerful. It activates the life-stimulating force of encircling and raises it to completion through the number seven.

Below are examples of encircling combined with the number seven in Jewish tradition.

- Seven circuits with Torah & dancing on *Simḥat Torah* in community.
- Seven circuits of the wedding ritual under the *Huppah.*
- Seven days of encircling on *Sukkot* - one on each of the first six days of *Sukkot* and then seven circuits on *Hoshanah Rabba,* the seventh day.
- Seven days of encircling *Yerikho* - six days of encircling one time, then seven circles on the final day to topple the walls of *Yerikho.*

About Ana B'khoaḥ

The *Ana B'khoaḥ* is a *piyyut* (spiritual poem) attributed to Rabbi Neḥunia ben HaKanah, in the second century CE. Many who attend Friday night Kabbalat Shabbat services will recognize it because *Ana B'khoaḥ* is chanted just before *Lekha Dodi* in many communities. It is the most familiar reference to the powerful 42-letter Name of God and is found in most Siddurim. In Sephardi, Mizraḥi and Hassidic (*Nussaḥ S'farad*) prayer books, the *Ana B'khoah* is also a part of the mourning liturgy.

Each line of the *Ana B'khoah* references one of the seven lower *S'firot* in the Kabbalistic Tree of Life. Each line holds a Divine Name within it to invoke the particular attribute associated with that *S'firah.*

Ana B'khoaḥ is composed of seven lines. Each line is made up of six words. The first letter of each of the 42 words make The Name of 42. In Gematria, 42 is Mem – Bet, מ"ב . *Mem Bet* is the acronym for מעשה בראשית - *Maaseh Bereshit* - which translates as the "act of creation," referencing creation in the Book of Genesis, the first book of Torah. This Name of 42 is known as the name that brings forward the fully potent, primordial, untainted, "Light of Eden" hidden away for the innocent in The Time That is Coming (*Olam Haba*).

The *Ana B'khoaḥ piyyut* is explained here for two reasons. First, it is an important part of the liturgy in *Sefer Maavar Yabbok*. In other words, *Sefer Maavar Yabbok's* end-of-life ritual includes reciting this prayer.

Second, the Name of 42 is hidden in the first letter of each of the words of the *Ana B'khoaḥ*. The Name of 42 is referenced again in *Seder Ha-Hakafot.* Because of the deep layers of connection between these two *piyyutim,* deciphering *Ana B'khoaḥ* is foundational to understanding the structure of *Seder Ha-Hakafot*.

Some will choose to practice *hakafot* only during pre-defined rituals. However, it is highly useful to cultivate a daily encircling practice, using the *Ana B'khoah.* Each of its seven lines accompanies one of the seven circuits. A regular practice of encircling, using the *Ana B'Khoah,* will make the end-of-life *hakafot* more potent.

ANA B'KHOAḤ LITURGY DECIPHERED

Translation by Rabbi Zalman Schachter-Shalomi, compiled by Rabbi T'mimah Ickovits

HESED Kindness, Expansion Limitlessness AVRAHAM, MIRYAM	חֶסֶד אב"ג ית"ץ	אָנָּא בְּכֹחַ גְּדֻלַּת יְמִינְךָ תַּתִּיר צְרוּרָה
ANa B'KHo-aH G'DuLaT Y'MiN'KHa TaTeeR TZ'RuRaH. *Source of Mercy, with loving strength, untie our tangles.*		
G'VURAH Discipline, Contraction, Containment YITZHAK, LEAH	גְּבוּרָה קר"ע שט"ן	קַבֵּל רִנַּת עַמְּךָ שַׂגְּבֵנוּ טַהֲרֵנוּ נוֹרָא
KaBeiL ReeNaT, AM'kHa SaG'VeiNu, TaHaReiNu NoRa. *Your chanting folk raise high, make pure, accept our song.*		
TIFERET Compassion, Harmonizing YAAKOV, HANNAH	תִּפְאֶרֶת נג"ד יכ"ש	נָא גִבּוֹר דּוֹרְשֵׁי יִחוּדְךָ כְּבָבַת שָׁמְרֵם
Na GeeBoR DoRSHeiY YeekḤooD'KHa K'VaVaT SHaM'ReiM. *Like your own eye, Lord keep us safe, who union seek with You.*		
NETZAH Perseverance, Focus, Victory MOSHE, RIVKAH	נֶצַח בט"ר צת"ג	בָּרְכֵם טַהֲרֵם רַחֲמֵם צִדְקָתְךָ תָּמִיד גָּמְלֵם
BaR'KHeiM TaHaReiM, RaHaMeiM TzeeD'Kat'KHa, TaMeeD GaM'LeiM. *Cleanse and bless us, infuse us ever, with loving Care.*		
HOD Glory, Humility AARON, SARAH	הוֹד חק"ב טנ"ע	חֲסִין קָדוֹשׁ בְּרוֹב טוּבְךָ נַהֵל עֲדָתֶךָ
ḤaSeeN KaDOSH, B'ROV TooV'KHa, NaHeiL ADaTeKHa. *Gracious Source, oh Holy Power, do guide Your folk.*		
YESOD Sexuality, Community YOSEPH, TAMAR	יְסוֹד יג"ל פז"ק	יָחִיד גֵּאֶה לְעַמְּךָ פְּנֵה זוֹכְרֵי קְדֻשָּׁתֶךָ
YaḤeed Gei-eh LaM'KHa P'Nay ZokhRei Ke'DooSHaTeKHa. *Sublime and Holy One, in your Great Goodness, lead Your flock.*		
SH'KHINAH [MALKHUT] Grounding, Rebirth, Release DAVID, RAḤEL	מַלְכוּת-שְׁכִינָה שק"ו צי"ת	שַׁוְעָתֵנוּ קַבֵּל וּשְׁמַע צַעֲקָתֵנוּ יוֹדֵעַ תַּעֲלוּמוֹת
SHaV'aTeiNu KaBeL, OOSH'Ma Tza-AKaTeiNU, YODei-A Ta-aLuMOT. *Receive our prayer, do hear our cry, who secrets knows.*		
Barookh shem kavod malkhuto l'olam va'ed *Through Time and Space your Glory Shines, Majestic One.*		בָּרוּךְ שֵׁם כְּבוֹד מַלְכוּתוֹ לְעוֹלָם וָעֶד:

Orchestrating Seder Ha-Hakafot

Now we prepare to dive into the ritual of *Seder Ha-Hakafot* as it appears in *Sefer Maavar Yabbok.*

After casketing, a series of prayers are read. The first is *uvin'soa haAron,* which is recited as the casket is moved to its next location.

After the deceased is relocated, the *Seder Ha-Hakafot* ritual can begin.

The ritual consists of the special liturgy of the *Seder Ha-Hakafot,* which is recited with each *hakafah* (encircling) around the *meitah/meit.* Additional recitations and acts may be added before each *hakafah,* including:

1. A portion of Psalm 91 is recited. (See page 23, large text denotes what to recite.)
2. Those present give *tzedakah* to honor the deceased and amplify their Heavenly merit.
3. The *Ana B'khoaḥ* prayer is recited by the prayer leader.
4. The thirteen attributes of mercy are recited by the prayer leader and answered to by the community with a special *yehi ratzon.*

You may include these additions or recite only the liturgy of the *Seder Ha-Hakafot.* Likewise, you can do the encircling with intention without any liturgy, which will provide a lift to the deceased.

For Whom do We Orchestrate Seder Ha-Hakafot?

Following Rabban Gamliel's example of equality in death, we recognize that all human beings are made in the Divine Image and are therefore important. We assert that people should not be valued only because of the perceived importance of their work or their social standing. It is therefore appropriate to honor all people with these *hakafot,* as the community sees fit.

Who does Seder Ha-Hakafot?

Hakafot around the deceased may be practiced by all those present: the *tohorah* team, family members and/or all community members present. The *hakafot* can be done more than one time. They offer an opportunity to express caring, loss, or something else, and to beautify the *mitzvah* of burying the dead.

When is Seder Ha-Hakafot Done

Seder Ha-Hakafot is done any time following *tohorah*, before burial. Some examples of when you might choose to perform the *hakafot* include:

1. Immediately following the *tohorah.*
2. In shul, before the *levaya*.
3. In the chapel at the cemetery, before or after the *hespeidim.*
4. On the way to the gravesite, making seven stops and performing one *hakafah* at each stop.
5. At the grave side, immediately before burial.

The image on the cover of this book is called "The Seven Circuits" by Bernard Picart (1673-1733) and can be found in the Royal Library of the Hague. It depicts people gathered to honor a recently passed loved one with *hakafot*.

Matbe'a (Structure) of Seder Ha-Hakafot

It appears that Rabbi Avraham Abulafia *z"l*, a great 13th century teacher of Ecstatic Kabbalah, influenced Rabbi Aharon Berekhiah's writing. [8] One of the sacred forms of *kavanot* (intentions) that Abulafia taught was that every spiritual process has three parts: a beginning, middle, and end.[9]

Likewise, each line of the words for the *hakafot* ritual contain a beginning, middle, and end.[10] Each weaves:

A. A salutation and a request carried on a Divine Name
B. Supplication for the deceased
C. A chorus asking for *kaparah* (expiation) and *rahamim* (maternal tenderness) on behalf of the deceased.

You will find these elements in the tables with the *Seder Ha-Hakafot* liturgy for the *hakafot* that begin on page 26 for women and page 38 for men. The columns with each element are labeled as follows:

Availing the Name of 42.
Behest supplications on behalf of the deceased.
Chorus reinforces the request.

A fourth column is added to show the Acronym for the specific Divine Name of God and the Attribute associated with the *S'firah*.

Read the prayers on the chart from right to left - A, B, C. The three parts are chanted during each *hakafah*. The fourth column is not recited but appears for reference.

---

8 Avraham Abulafia went to visit the Pope. Anticipating Abulafia's arrival, the Pope built gallows to hang him. Upon his arrival Abulafia was captured and thrown into a dungeon. That night the Pope mysteriously died. Abulafia was released and spent years teaching in Italy. Moshe Idel PhD. Messianic Mystics class 2002 UCLA.

9 *Rosh, Tokh, v'Sof*; ראש,תוך,וסוף. Moshe Idel PhD, 2002.

10 *Sefer Maavar Yabbok* attributes this ritual to "Hillel, the Elder," who is associated with the development of Mishnah. He is famous for two sayings, "If I am not for myself, who will be for me? And being only myself, what am I?"

Guidelines:

- Hebrew derived from Torah is maintained as originally written.
- Liturgy from *Maavar Yabbok* Hebrew is shown first in the feminine, then in the original masculine.
- Pages containing two columns – Hebrew on the right and English translation on the left—are instructions from *Maavar Yabbok.*
- Three-column charts are prayers to be recited from *Maavar Yabbok* - Hebrew text on the right, transliteration in the center, translation on the left.
- Throughout, [Brackets] are the author's interpretation; (parentheses) are explanations provided by Aharon Berekhiah in *Sefer Maavar Yabbok.*

Kavanot (Kabbalistic Intentions) for Hakafot

The secret of seven has extraordinary kabbalistic significance and resonates with the seven lower *s'firot* from the *eitz hayyim,* or Tree of Life.

Each *hakafah* invites contemplation of a unique Divine Attribute from the "Secret of Seven" to be cultivated by the community.

- First circle – *Ḥesed;* Lovingkindness
- Second circle – *G'vurah;* Boundary
- Third circle – *Tiferet;* Beauty
- Fourth circle – *Netzaḥ;* Eternity, Victory
- Fifth circle – *Hod;* Gratitude, Pause
- Sixth circle – *Yesod;* Foundation, Community, Intimany
- Seventh circle – *Sh'khinah* [*Malkhut*]; Sovereignty, The Great Receiving

A unique six-letter Name of God references each of the above attributes in both the *Ana B'Khoaḥ* and the *Seder Ha-Hakafot.*

Now we step into the service, taken from *Sefer Maavar Yabbok,* for the *Seder Ha-Hakafot.*

The service for women begins on page 22.

The service for men begins on page 34.

Seder Ha-Hakafot for Women[11]

This is a translation of the Introduction to *Seder Ha-Hakafot* in *Maavar Yabbok* adapted for use by women. It is not recited.

Tremendous ease [is cultivated] for the *nefesh* of the deceased through these Seven *hakafot* and their *kavanot*. [See] Chapter 17, Part 3 and Chapter 30, Part 5 [of *Siftay Tzedek*.]

נייחא גדולה לנפש הנפטרת בשבע הקפות וכוונתם מתבאר בפרק י"ז מאמר ג' ועוד בפרק ל' מאמר ה':

This is the order that was found in *Divrei Ḥakhamim* [Writings of the Sages] about the Great *Reḥitzah* [washing] attributed to Hillel the Elder.

וזהו סדר כפי הנמצא בדברי חכמים ברחיצה הגדולה המיוחסת להלל הזקן:

As part of each *hakafah* you will recite:

בכל הקפה יאמר:

"*Yoshev b'seter elyon*" until "*Ki atah Hashem Maḥsi*" (*Psalm* 91) and give each time at least one coin for *tzedakah* for the deceased or set it aside in her purse [to do more] to atone for her soul.

"יושב בסתר עליון" עד "כי אתה ה' מחסי..." סימן צ"א, ויתן בכל פעם לפחות פרוטה לצדקה על המתה או יפרישנו בכיסו לכפרת נפשה.

Psalms and readings to precede Seder Ha-Hakafot begin on the next page.

11 *Sefer Maavar Yabbok, Siftay Tzedek - Perek Zayin* - Chapter 7 - Vilna - page *nun-gimel*: p. 106, *Ahavat Shalom* - page קכו (126)

תהילים צ"א – Psalm 91—Recite until the break:

Yosheiv b'seiter elyon,
b'tzel shadai yitlonan:
*Omar la-**Adonai**, maḥsi oom'tzudati*
Eloha evtah bo:
Kee hoo yatzil'kha mepah yakoosh
midever havot:
b'evrato yasekh lakh v'taḥat k'nafav
teḥseh tzinah v'soheirah amito:
Lo tirah mipaḥad liylah, meihetz
ya-oof yomam:
midever ba-ofel yahalokh,
meketev yashoor tzaharain:
Yipol mitzid'kha elef oor'vavah
miminekha, elekha lo yigash:
rak b'eynekha tabit
v'shilumat r'shaiim tir-eh:
*Ki atah **Adonai***
maḥsi elyon samta m'onekha:

יֹשֵׁב בְּסֵתֶר עֶלְיוֹן
בְּצֵל שַׁדַּי יִתְלוֹנָן:
אֹמַר לַיהוָה אדני יאהדונהי מַחְסִי וּמְצוּדָתִי
אֱלֹהַי אֶבְטַח־בּוֹ:
כִּי הוּא יַצִּילְךָ מִפַּח יָקוּשׁ מִדֶּבֶר הַוּוֹת:
בְּאֶבְרָתוֹ | יָסֶךְ לָךְ וְתַחַת־כְּנָפָיו
תֶּחְסֶה צִנָּה וְסֹחֵרָה אֲמִתּוֹ:
לֹא־תִירָא מִפַּחַד לָיְלָה מֵחֵץ
יָעוּף יוֹמָם:
מִדֶּבֶר בָּאֹפֶל יַהֲלֹךְ מִקֶּטֶב
יָשׁוּד צָהֳרָיִם:
יִפֹּל מִצִּדְּךָ | אֶלֶף וּרְבָבָה מִימִינֶךָ
אֵלֶיךָ לֹא יִגָּשׁ:
רַק בְּעֵינֶיךָ תַבִּיט
וְשִׁלֻּמַת רְשָׁעִים תִּרְאֶה:
כִּי־אַתָּה יְהוָה אדני יאהדונהי
מַחְסִי עֶלְיוֹן שַׂמְתָּ מְעוֹנֶךָ:

Lo t'ooneh elekha ra-ah
v'nega lo yikrav b'ohalekha:
Ki mal'akh-av y'tzaveh lakh lish'mar'kha
b'khol d'rakheikha:
Al kapaiim yisa-oonkha pen tigof
ba-even rag'lekha:
Al shaḥal vapiten tidrokh
tirmos k'fir v'tanin:
kei vi ḥashak, va-afal'teihu
asagveihu key yada Sh'mi:
Yik'ra-eini v'eh-ehneihu emo anokhi v'tzarah
ahal'tzeihu va-akhab'deihu:
Orekh yamim as'bieihu v'areihu biy'shuati:

לֹא־תְאֻנֶּה אֵלֶיךָ רָעָה
וְנֶגַע לֹא־יִקְרַב בְּאָהֳלֶךָ:
כִּי מַלְאָכָיו יְצַוֶּה־לָּךְ לִשְׁמָרְךָ
בְּכָל־דְּרָכֶיךָ:
עַל־כַּפַּיִם יִשָּׂאוּנְךָ פֶּן־תִּגֹּף בָּאֶבֶן רַגְלֶךָ:
עַל־שַׁחַל וָפֶתֶן תִּדְרֹךְ
תִּרְמֹס כְּפִיר וְתַנִּין:
כִּי בִי חָשַׁק וַאֲפַלְּטֵהוּ
אֲשַׂגְּבֵהוּ כִּי־יָדַע שְׁמִי:
יִקְרָאֵנִי | וְאֶעֱנֵהוּ עִמּוֹ־אָנֹכִי
בְצָרָה אֲחַלְּצֵהוּ וַאֲכַבְּדֵהוּ:
אֹרֶךְ יָמִים אַשְׂבִּיעֵהוּ וְאַרְאֵהוּ בִּישׁוּעָתִי:

Psalm 91

Translation by Rabbi Zalman Schachter-Shalomi.

(A song against evil spirits)

In concealment You dwell,
Most High, Almighty,
You linger in the shadow.

I say to You YAH
You are both my safe haven,

My bastion holding me.
I must trust You my G!D.

You save me from entrapment,
from putrid scourge.

You cover me under Your shelter.
You keep me safe under
Your Wings.
I am protected by Your truth.

(I am assured by You.)
Do not panic
facing night's terror,
a bullet shot in broad daylight,
a blight creeping in the murky dark,
a wasting plague at high noon.

You will not be harmed
though a thousand fall near you
a myriad at your right hand.

You just look steadfastly ahead
and you will see
how malice will
get its rebuke.

Yes, You, YAH are my defense.
I am at home with You,
high beyond reach.
(You assure me.)

No mishap will befall you.
Your tent will be safe from harm.
Angels are appointed to care
and watch over you
wherever you are.

They will bear you high
on their hands.
You will not strike your foot
against a stone.
Snakes and wildcats
will avoid you.
Lions and serpents
will get out of your way.

(You assure me.)
Because you long for Me
I will rescue you.
I will raise you up
because you know My Name.
When you call Me
I will answer you.
I will free you and esteem you.

I will make you content
with your lifespan
and I will have you witness
how I bring deliverance.

Place tzedakah in receptacle and recite:

ותאמר:

Here I give this money as *tzedakah* on behalf of all Yisrael and for "*Plonit*," this deceased woman, [advocating] for her soul to rest in *Gan Eden*.

Hareini notenet prutah zoo letz'dakah al kol Yisra-el v'al "Plonit" zot hanifteret lim'nuḥat nishmatah b'Gan Eden.

הֲרֵינִי נוֹתֶנֶת פְּרוּטָה זוּ לִצְדָקָה
עַל כָּל יִשְׂרָאֵל וְעַל "פְּלוֹנִית"
זֹאת הַנִּפְטֶרֶת לִמְנוּחַת
נִשְׁמָתָהּ בְּגַן עֵדֶן:

For each and every *hakafah*, when the prayer leader exits the line, he or she will say the *Ana B'khoah* and I have also found that it's good to say the Thirteen Attributes. And when the prayer leader [begins the Thirteen Attributes] by saying *V'yaavor* (and He passed), which [initiates] the arousal of compassion, the people present will say:

ובכל הקפה אחת שיצא החזן מן השורה יאמר אנא בכח וגו' ומצאתי כי טוב לומר י"ג מדות וכשהחזן אומר ויעבור שאז הוא התעוררות הרחמים יאמרו כל העם:

May it be Your Will, Adonai, our *Elohim* and *Elohim* of our ancestors to offer maternal mercy to "*Plonit*" this woman, now free from all worldly obligations, that all her transgressions and iniquities be pardoned. Adonai Adonai, *Eil* Maternally Tender and Gracious.

Y'hi ratzon milfanekha Adonai Eloheinu v'Elohei Avoteinu v'Emoteinu shet'raḥeim al "Plonit" zot hanifteret, v'timḥol lah kol p'sha-ehah va-avonoteha, Adonai Adonai Eil raḥum v'ḥanun.

יְהִי רָצוֹן מִלְּפָנֶיךָ
יְהֹוָאדֹנָי יאהדונהי אֱלֹהֵינוּ
וֵאלֹהֵי אֲבוֹתֵינוּ וְאִמּוֹתֵינוּ
שֶׁתְּרַחֵם עַל "פְּלוֹנִית"
זֹאת הַנִּפְטֶרֶת וְתִמְחוֹל
לָהּ כָּל פְּשָׁעֶיהָ וַעֲוֹנוֹתֶיהָ,
יְהֹוָאדֹנָי יאהדונהי יְהֹוָאדֹנָי יאהדונהי
אֵל רַחוּם וְחַנּוּן.

Give the *prootot* [coinage, money] to the impoverished, and if they are not to be found, go and look for them within twenty-four hours.

יתנו הפרוטות לעניים אז אם אינם מצויים שם יחזר אחריהם תוך כ"ד שעות.

In *Eretz Israel*, it is the custom to cut up a gold coin into fine pieces and to place it upon her—with silver and copper. This was the practice for a well-respected person.

בא"י נוהגים לחתוך א' מטבע זהב כגון ציקינ"ו לחתיכות דקות להשים אותו עליה עם כסף ונחשת וזה לאדם גדול:

And these are the *hakafot* according to the order of the Name of 42:

ואלו הם ההקפות על סדר שם של מ"ב:

Seder Ha-Hakafot for Women

Recite the liturgy for ***Seder Ha-Hakafot,*** starting **from right to left through columns A) Availing, B) Behest and C) Chorus**. Repeat the same order for all *hakafot* on the following pages.

HESED, LOVINGKINDNESS - Hakafah 1			
Acronym and Attribute	Chorus	Behest	Availing Name of 42
אב"ג ית"ץ חֶסֶד	וְיִשְׁלַח כַּפָּרָה לְאַשְׁמָתָהּ וְיִתֵּן אֵלֶיהָ רַחֲמֶיהָ:	וְיִפְתַּח לָהּ מְקוֹם קִבְרֵי אֲבוֹתֶיהָ	אֵל בָּרוּךְ גָּדוֹל יִרְאֶה תֹּום צִדְקוֹתֶיהָ
ḤESED	*V'yishlaḥ Kaparah L'Ashmatah, V'yiten Eiley-ha Raḥamayha*	*V'Yiftaḥ Lah M'kom Kivray Avoteyha*	***E**il **B**arukh **G**adol **Y**ir-eh **T**om **Tz**idkotey-ha*
Kindness Expansion Unlimited	Send forgiveness for remaining guilt and give to her the tenderness she built.	Open her space in the graves of her ancestors.	***Eil,*** Praised and Great G!D, See the wholesomeness of her innocence!

Hesed spreads expansively, like water

G'VURAH, BOUNDARY - Hakafah 2			
Acronym and Attribute	Chorus	Behest	Availing Name of 42
קר"ע שט"ן גְּבוּרָה	וְיִשְׁלַח כַּפָּרָה לְאַשְׁמָתָהּ וְיִתֵּן אֵלֶיהָ רַחֲמֶיהָ:	וְחַלְּצֶיהָ פֶּן תְּאָכְלֶיהָ לַהַט הַחֶרֶב בְּאִשּׁוֹ וְתִכָּנֵס לְגַן עֲדָנֶיהָ וְלֹא יִזָּכְרוּ עוֹד עֲוֹנֶיהָ	קָדוֹשׁ רַחוּם עֶלְיוֹן שׁוּר טוֹהַר נַפְשָׁהּ
G'VURAH	*V'yishlaḥ Kaparah L'Ashmatah, V'yiten Eiley-ha Raḥamayha*	*V'ḥal'tzeiha, pen t'akh'leiha lahat haḥerev b'eesho v'tikaneis l'gan od-neha v'lo yizkiru od avoneyha:*	***K**adosh **R**ahum **E**lyon **Sh**ur **T**ohar **N**afshah*
Discipline Contract Membrane Discernment Nature	Send forgiveness for remaining guilt and give to her the tenderness she built.	Save her, let her not be consumed by flaming sword's fire. Let her arrive into Eden, with no memory of iniquity.	Holy Merciful One on high, observe the purity of her soul.

G'vurah sets boundaries, like Fire.

TIFERET, BEAUTY, BALANCE - Hakafah 3

Acronym and Attribute	Chorus	Behest	Availing Name of 42
נג"ד יכ"ש **תִּפְאֶרֶת**	וְיִשְׁלַח כַּפָּרָה לְאַשְׁמָתָהּ וְיִתֵּן אֵלֶיהָ רַחֲמֶיהָ:	וְתִזְכֶּה לִכְּנֵס לְנוֹגַהּ וְעָנָן מְסֻכָּתָהּ וּבוֹ תַּעֲלֶה וְלֹא תֵרֵד וְלֹא יִזָּכֵר לָהּ עָוֹן וָמֶרֶד	נָא גָדוֹל דָגוּל יְגַדֵּל כֹּחַ שְׁמִירָתָהּ
TIFERET	*V'yishlaḥ Kaparah L'Ashmatah, V'yiten Eiley-ha Raḥameyha*	*V'tizkeh lica-neis l'nogah v'anan m'sukatah, oovo ta-aleh v'lo teireid, v'lo yizakheir la avon va-mered*	*Na **G**adol **D**agool **Y**'gadeil Ko'ah **Sh**'mira-ta*
Compassion Harmony Balance Maternal Mercy	Send forgiveness for remaining guilt and give to her the tenderness she built.	She will merit entry into Divine radiance, protected by cloud cover; in it she will ascend, and never fall, with iniquity or offense not recalled.	Please, Great Exalted (One), amplify the powers of her protectors.

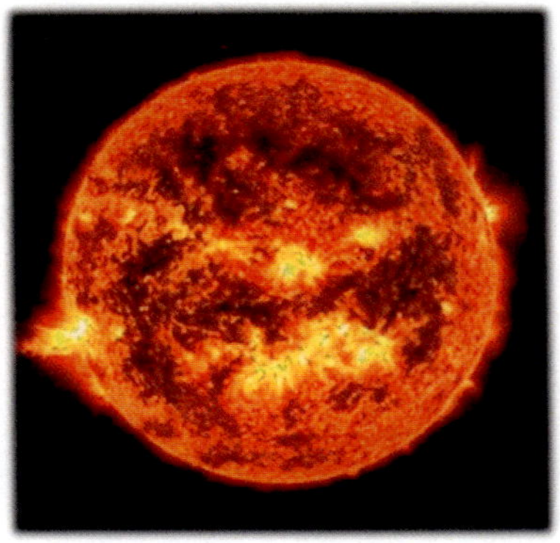

The Sun, and its balanced warmth is a classical representation of Tiferet from the Holy Zohar

NETZAH, ETERNITY, VICTORY - Hakafah 4			
Acronym and Attribute	Chorus	Behest	Availing Name of 42
בט"ר צת"ג **נֵצַח**	וְיִשְׁלַח כַּפָּרָה לְאַשְׁמָתָהּ וְיִתֵּן אֵלֶיהָ רַחֲמֶיהָ:	וּמִנַּחַל עֲדָנֶךָ תַּשְׁקֶהָ וְיִפָּתְחוּ לָהּ שַׁעֲרֵי יְרוּשָׁלַיִם וּמִיכָאֵל יַקְרִיבָהּ לִפְנֵי שׁוֹכֵן שָׁמַיִם	בְּרַחֲמֵי טָהוֹר רַחֲמֶהָ צִדְקָהּ תָּמִיד גָּמְלֶהָ
NETZAḤ	*V'yishlaḥ Kaparah L'Ashmatah, V'yiten Eiley-ha Raḥamayha*	*Oominaḥal adanekha tash'keiha v'yift'ḥu lah sha-arei Y'rushalyim, ooMikha-el yak'rivah lifnei Shokhen Shamayim*	***B****'raḥamei* ***T****ahor* ***R****aḥameiha* ***Tz****'dakah,* ***T****amid,* ***G****am'leiha*
Sustain Focus Eternal Victory	Send forgiveness for remaining guilt and give to her the tenderness she built.	Through the river of Your Eden, quench her. Open the gates of *Yerushalayim* for her; Mikha'el will bring her close to the "*Shokhen Shamayim*," the One who dwells in Heaven.	With pure compassion, be tender with her. See her merit, perpetually.

Netzah is tenacious, just like this flower. It lives staying the course in the hot dry desert, managing to locate adequate water and nourishment.

HOD, GRATITUDE, WAITING - Hakafah 5			
Acronym and Attribute	Chorus	Behest	Availing Name of 42
חזק"ב טנ"ע הוד	וְיִשְׁלַח כַּפָּרָה לְאַשְׁמָתָה וְיִתֵּן אֵלֶיהָ רַחֲמֶיהָ:	וּבֵית מִקְדָּשׁ וְאַפִּרְיוֹן יִפְתְּחוּ לָה בְּרָצוֹן וּמִכָאֵל יַכְנִיסֶהָ בְּשָׂשׂוֹן בְּשִׂמְחָה וּבְשָׂשׂוֹן	חַי קָדוֹשׁ בָּרוּךְ טְהֵר נַפְשָׁה עֶלְיוֹן
HOD	*V'yishlaḥ Kaparah L'Ashmatah, V'yiten Eiley-ha Raḥameyha*	*Ooveit Mik'dash, v'Apiryon, Yifat'ḥu Lah B'ratzon, ooMikha-el, Yakh'niseiha B'Sason, B'Simḥah oov'Sason.*	***Ḥ**ai **K**adosh, **B**arukh, **T**'heir, **N**af'shah **E**lyon*
Gratitude, Waiting Waits for impetus,	Send forgiveness for remaining guilt and give to her the tenderness she built.	The Temple and High Heavens will burst open with deep desire. Mikha'el will escort her in - with glee, with joy, with glee.	Living, Holy, and Blessed One, purify her heavenly soul.

Hod knows when to pause and allow, like this mama cat does when her kittens need nourishment.

YESOD, FOUNDATION, INTIMACY - Hakafah 6			
Acronym and Attribute	Chorus	Behest	Availing Name of 42
יג"ל פז"ק יסוד	וְיִשְׁלַח כַּפָּרָה לְאַשְׁמָתָה וְיִתֵּן אֵלֶיהָ רַחֲמֶיהָ:	וְעַל מִזְבַּח הַקָּדוֹשׁ נִשְׁמָתָהּ תִּהְיֶה נִצֶּבֶת וּמִפִּי עֶלְיוֹן שָׁם תִּהְיֶה מְבוֹרֶכֶת	יָהּ גַּלֵּה לְבַת פְּדוּתֶךָ זָךְ קָדוֹשׁ
YESOD	*V'yishlaḥ Kaparah L'Ashmatah, V'yiten Eiley-ha Raḥameyha*	*V'al mizbaḥ hakadosh nishmatah tih'yeh nitzevet, oomi-pi elyon sham tih'yeh m'vorekhet*	***YAH G****alei* ***L****abat* ***P****'dootekha,* ***Z****akh* ***K****adosh*
Foundation Intimacy	Send forgiveness for remaining guilt and give to her the tenderness she built.	On the holy altar, her *neshamah* will stand, and from Heavenly Mouth, there, she will be blessed.	**YAH**, reveal to Your redeemed daughter, holy clarity.

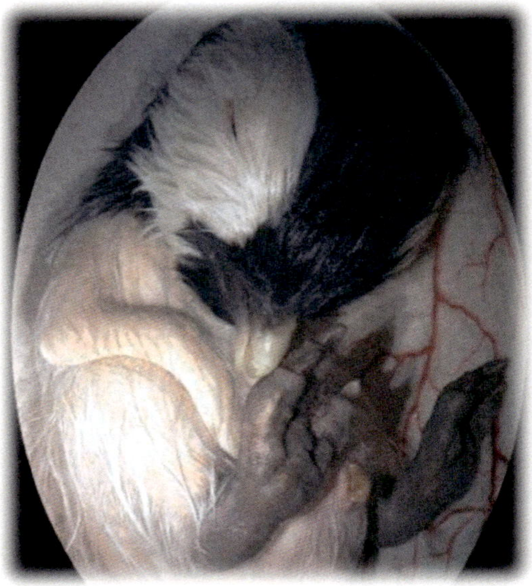

Yesod resonates intimacy, sexuality and fertility. The bird in gestation is being nourished with in the egg, highlights the deep beauty of this most organic process.

SH'KHINAH, SOVEREIGNTY- Hakafah 7			
Acronym and Attribute	Chorus	Behest	Availing Name of 42
שׁקּ"ו צי"ת מלכות	וְיִשְׁלַח כַּפָּרָה לְנִשְׁמָתָהּ וְיִתֵּן אֵלֶיהָ רַחֲמֶיהָ:	יִהְיֶה לְנֶפֶשׁ זֶה מַחֲזִיק וְתוֹמֵךְ וּבַעֲרָבוֹת לְפָנֶךָ יְשַׁמֵּשׁ וְיוֹמָם וְלַיְלָה לֹא יָמוּשׁ	שׁוֹכֵן קֶדֶם וּמֵאָז צֶדֶק יוֹשֶׁר תּוֹמֶךְ
SH'KHINAH [MALKHUT]	*V'yishlaḥ Kaparah L'Ashmatah, V'yiten Eiley-ha Raḥameyha*	*Yih'yeh l'nefesh zeh maḥazik v'tomeikh oova-aravot l'fanekha y'shameish v'yomam v'liyla lo yamush*	***Sh**okhen **K**edem **Oo**mei-az, **T**zedek **Y**osher **T**oomekh*
Majesty	Send forgiveness for remaining guilt and give to her the tenderness she built.	There will be strengthening and wholesomeness for this *nefesh*. And In the heavens she will use them day and night, never ceasing.	Primordial Dweller, from earliest times till now, direct the virtuous integrity of Your purity.

This new lamb is a sovereign conscious being once born into the world. No one can eat for her, move for her or get sick for her. Sh'khinah is Sovereingty.

Through Time and Space your Glory Shines, Majestic One.	*Barookh shem k'vod malkhuto l'olam va'ed*	בָּרוּךְ שֵׁם כְּבוֹד מַלְכוּתוֹ לְעוֹלָם וָעֶד:

After the *hakafot,* chant the following verse:

And to the children of	*v'livnei hafilagshim*	וְלִבְנֵי הַפִּילַגְשִׁים
Avraham's concubines,	*asher l'Avraham*	אֲשֶׁר לְאַבְרָהָם
Avraham gave gifts.[12]	*natan Avraham matanot*	נָתַן אַבְרָהָם מַתָּנֹת

It is good to do this at the cemetery after saying *tzidduk hadin,* or at the home of the *meitah* before lifting her up and carrying her (to her final resting place)[13].

---

[12] The Torah's concern for a concubine who had a child with Avraham reminds us of the need for inclusivity; to care for all mourners with comfort and kindness, especially where family matters get blurry or for relatives who are not part of the "inner" circle or are not Jewish.

[13] *Maavar Yabbok* Vilna Version 106 נד : *Ahavat Shalom* Version קכו

Seder Ha-Hakafot for Men[14]

We now move to the direct translation of the Introduction to *Seder Ha-Hakafot* in *Maavar Yabbok*. The following are instructions and are not recited.

נייחא גדולה לנפש הנפטר בשבע הקפות וכוונתם מתבאר בפרק י"ז מאמר ג' ועוד בפרק ל' מאמר ה':

Tremendous ease [is cultivated] for the *nefesh* of the deceased through these Seven *hakafot* and their *kavanot*. [See] Chapter 17 part 3 and chapter 30 part 5 [of *Siftay Tzedek*.]

וזהו סדר כפי הנמצא בדברי חכמים ברחיצה הגדולה המיוחסת להלל הזקן:

This is the order that was found in *Divrei Ḥakhamim* [Writings of the Sages] about the Great *Reḥitza* [washing] attributed to Hillel the Elder.

בכל הקפה יאמר:

"יושב בסתר עליון" עד "כי אתה ה' מחסי..." סימן צ"א, ויתן בכל פעם לפחות פרוטה לצדקה על המת או יפרישנו בכיסו לכפרת נפשו

As part of each and every *hakafah*, you will recite*:*

Chant Psalm 91, beginning from "*Yoshev b'seter elyon*" until "*Ki atah Hashem Maḥsi*". (*Siman* 91) and give each time at least one coin for *tzedakah* for the deceased or set it aside in his purse [to do more] to atone for his soul.

Psalms and readings to precede Seder Ha-Hakafot begin on the next page.

[14] *Siftay Tzedek - Perek Zayin* - Chapter 7 - Vilna - page *nun-gimel*: p. 106, *Ahavat Shalom* - page *kuf chaf vav* - p. 126

תהילים צ"א – Psalm 91—Recite until the break:

Yosheiv b'seiter elyon,	יֹשֵׁב בְּסֵתֶר עֶלְיוֹן
b'tzel shadai yitlonan:	בְּצֵל שַׁדַּי יִתְלוֹנָן׃
*Omar la-**Adonai**, maḥsi oom'tzudati*	אֹמַר לַיהֹוָה יאהדונהי מַחְסִי וּמְצוּדָתִי
Eloha evtah bo:	אֱלֹהַי אֶבְטַח־בּוֹ׃
Kee hoo yatzil'kha mepah yakoosh	כִּי הוּא יַצִּילְךָ מִפַּח יָקוּשׁ מִדֶּבֶר הַוּוֹת׃
midever havot:	
b'evrato yasekh lakh v'taḥat k'nafav	בְּאֶבְרָתוֹ ׀ יָסֶךְ לָךְ וְתַחַת־כְּנָפָיו
teḥseh tzinah v'soheirah amito:	תֶּחְסֶה צִנָּה וְסֹחֵרָה אֲמִתּוֹ׃
Lo tirah mipaḥad liylah, meihetz	לֹא־תִירָא מִפַּחַד לָיְלָה מֵחֵץ
ya-oof yomam:	יָעוּף יוֹמָם׃
midever ba-ofel yahalokh,	מִדֶּבֶר בָּאֹפֶל יַהֲלֹךְ מִקֶּטֶב
meketev yashoor tzaharain:	יָשׁוּד צָהֳרָיִם׃
Yipol mitzid'kha elef oor'vavah	יִפֹּל מִצִּדְּךָ ׀ אֶלֶף וּרְבָבָה מִימִינֶךָ
miminekha, elekha lo yigash:	אֵלֶיךָ לֹא יִגָּשׁ׃
rak b'eynekha tabit	רַק בְּעֵינֶיךָ תַבִּיט
v'shilumat r'shaiim tir-eh:	וְשִׁלֻּמַת רְשָׁעִים תִּרְאֶה׃
*Ki atah **Adonai***	כִּי־אַתָּה יְהֹוָה יאהדונהי
maḥsi elyon samta m'onekha:	מַחְסִי עֶלְיוֹן שַׂמְתָּ מְעוֹנֶךָ׃

Lo t'ooneh elekha ra-ah	לֹא־תְאֻנֶּה אֵלֶיךָ רָעָה
v'nega lo yikrav b'ohalekha:	וְנֶגַע לֹא־יִקְרַב בְּאָהֳלֶךָ׃
Ki mal'akh-av y'tzaveh lakh lish'mar'kha	כִּי מַלְאָכָיו יְצַוֶּה־לָּךְ לִשְׁמָרְךָ
b'khol d'rakheikha:	בְּכָל־דְּרָכֶיךָ׃
Al kapaiim yisa-oonkha pen tigof	עַל־כַּפַּיִם יִשָּׂאוּנְךָ פֶּן־תִּגֹּף בָּאֶבֶן רַגְלֶךָ׃
ba-even rag'lekha:	
Al shaḥal vapiten tidrokh	עַל־שַׁחַל וָפֶתֶן תִּדְרֹךְ
tirmos k'fir v'tanin:	תִּרְמֹס כְּפִיר וְתַנִּין׃
kei vi ḥashak, va-afal'teihu	כִּי בִי חָשַׁק וַאֲפַלְּטֵהוּ
asagveihu key yada Sh'mi:	אֲשַׂגְּבֵהוּ כִּי־יָדַע שְׁמִי׃
Yik'ra-eini v'eh-ehneihu emo anokhi v'tzarah	יִקְרָאֵנִי ׀ וְאֶעֱנֵהוּ עִמּוֹ־אָנֹכִי
ahal'tzeihu va-akhab'deihu:	בְצָרָה אֲחַלְּצֵהוּ וַאֲכַבְּדֵהוּ׃
Orekh yamim as'bieihu v'areihu biy'shuati:	אֹרֶךְ יָמִים אַשְׂבִּיעֵהוּ וְאַרְאֵהוּ בִּישׁוּעָתִי׃

Psalm 91

Translation by Rabbi Zalman Schachter-Shalomi.

(A song against evil spirits)

In concealment You dwell,
Most High, Almighty,
You linger in the shadow.

I say to You YAH
You are both my safe haven,

My bastion holding me.
I must trust You my G!D.

You save me from entrapment,
from putrid scourge.

You cover me under Your shelter.
You keep me safe under
Your Wings.
I am protected by Your truth.

(I am assured by You.)
Do not panic
facing night's terror,
a bullet shot in broad daylight,
a blight creeping in the murky dark,
a wasting plague at high noon.

You will not be harmed
though a thousand fall near you
a myriad at your right hand.

You just look steadfastly ahead
and you will see
how malice will
get its rebuke.

Yes, You, YAH are my defense.
I am at home with You,
high beyond reach.
(You assure me.)

No mishap will befall you.
Your tent will be safe from harm.
Angels are appointed to care
and watch over you
wherever you are.

They will bear you high
on their hands.
You will not strike your foot
against a stone.
Snakes and wildcats
will avoid you.
Lions and serpents
will get out of your way.

(You assure me.)
Because you long for Me
I will rescue you.
I will raise you up
because you know My Name.
When you call Me
I will answer you.
I will free you and esteem you.

I will make you content
with your lifespan
and I will have you witness
how I bring deliverance.

Place tzedakah in receptacle and recite:

ויאמר:

Here I give this money as *tzedakah* on behalf of all Yisrael and for *"Ploni,"* this deceased man, [advocating] for his soul to rest in *Gan Eden.*

Hareini noten prutah zoo letz'dakah al kol Yisra-el v'al "Ploni" zeh haniftar lim'nuḥat nishmato b'Gan Eden.

הֲרֵינִי נוֹתֵן פְּרוּטָה זוּ לִצְדָקָה עַל כָּל יִשְׂרָאֵל וְעַל "פְּלוֹנִי" זֶה הַנִּפְטָר לִמְנוּחַת נִשְׁמָתוֹ בְּגַן עֵדֶן:

For each and every *hakafah*, when the prayer leader exits the line, he or she will say the *Ana B'khoah* and I have also found that it's good to say the Thirteen Attributes. And when the prayer leader [begins the Thirteen Attributes] by saying *V'yaavor* (and He passed), which [initiates] the arousal of compassion, the people present will say:

ובכל הקפה אחת שיצא החזן מן השורה יאמר אנא בכח וגו' ומצאתי כי טוב לומר י"ג מדות וכשהחזן אומר ויעבור שאז הוא התעוררות הרחמים יאמרו כל העם:

May it be Your Will, **Adonai**, our ***Elohim*** and ***Elohim*** of our ancestors to offer maternal mercy to *"Plony"* this man, now free from all worldly obligations, that all his transgressions and iniquities be pardoned. **Adonai Adonai**, ***Eil*** Merciful and Gracious.

Y'hi ratzon milfanekha ***Adonai Eloheinu*** *v'****Elohei*** *Avoteinu v'Emoteinu shet'raheim al "Plony" zeh hanifter, v'timhol lo kol p'sha-av va-avonotav,* ***Adonai Adonai Eil*** *raḥum v'ḥanun.*

יְהִי רָצוֹן מִלְּפָנֶיךָ יהוהאדני יאהדונהי אֱלֹהֵינוּ וֵאלֹהֵי אֲבוֹתֵינוּ וְאִמּוֹתֵינוּ שֶׁתְּרַחֵם עַל "פְּלוֹנִי" זֶה הַנִּפְטָר וְתִמְחוֹל לוֹ כָּל פְּשָׁעָיו וַעֲוֹנוֹתָיו, יהוהאדני יאהדונהי יהוהאדני יאהדונהי אֵל רַחוּם וְחַנּוּן.

Give the *prootot* (coinage, money) to the impoverished, and if they are not to be found, go and look for them within twenty-four hours.

יתנו הפרוטות לעניים אז אם אינם מצויים שם יחזור אחריהם תוך כ"ד שעות.

In *Eretz Israel*, it is the custom to cut up a gold coin into fine pieces and to place it upon him - with silver and copper . This was the practice for a well-respected person.

בא"י נוהגים לחתוך א' מטבע זהב כגון ציקינ"ו לחתיכות דקות להשים אותו עליו עם כסף ונחשת וזה לאדם גדול:

And these are the *hakafot* according to the order of the Name of 42:

ואלו הם ההקפות על סדר שם של מ"ב:

Seder Ha-Hakafot for Men

Recite the liturgy for ***Seder Ha-Hakafot,*** starting **from right to left through columns A) Availing, B) Behest and C) Chorus**. Repeat the same order for all *hakafot* on the following pages.

ḤESED, GRACE - Hakafah 1			
Acronym and Attribute	Chorus	Behest	Availing Name of 42
אַב"ג יתַ"ץ חֶסֶד	וְיִשְׁלַח כַּפָּרָה לְאַשְׁמָתוֹ וְיִתֵּן אֵלָיו רַחֲמָיו:	וְיִפְתַּח לוֹ מְקוֹם קִבְרֵי אֲבוֹתָיו	**אֵל בָּרוּךְ גָּדוֹל יִרְאֶה תֹּום צִדְקוֹתָיו**
ḤESED	*V'yishlah Kaparaḥ L'Ashmato, V'yiten Eilav Raḥamav*	*V'Yiftaḥ Lo M'kom Kivray Avotav*	***E**il **B**arukh **G**adol **Y**ir-eh **T**om **Tz**idkotav*
Kindness Expansion Unlimited	Send forgiveness for remaining guilt and give to him the tenderness he built.	Open his space in the graves of his ancestors.	***Eil,*** Praised and Great G!D, See the wholesomeness of his innocence!

Water's expansive nature and life-giving force, is a classical model of Hesed.

G'VURAH, STRENGTH - Hakafah 2			
Acronym and Attribute	Chorus	Behest	Availing Name of 42
קר"ע שט"ן גְּבוּרָה	וְיִשְׁלַח כַּפָּרָה לַאֲשְׁמָתוֹ וְיִתֵּן אֵלָיו רַחֲמָיו:	וְחַלְּצֵהוּ פֶּן תְּאָכְלֵהוּ לַהַט הַחֶרֶב בְּאִשּׁוֹ וְיִכָּנֵס לְגַן עֲדָנָיו וְלֹא יִזָּכְרוּ עוֹד עֲוֹנָיו	קָדוֹשׁ רַחוּם עֶלְיוֹן שׁוֹר טוֹהַר נַפְשׁוֹ
G'VURAH	*V'yishlaḥ Kaparah L'Ashmato, V'yiten Eilav Raḥamav*	*V'ḥaltzeihu pen t'akhleihu lahat ha-ḥerev b'eesho v'yikaneis l'gan edanav v'lo yizkh'ru od avonotav*	***K**adosh **R**ahum **E**lyon **Sh**ur **T**ohar **N**afsho*
Discipline Contract Membrane Discern Nature	Send forgiveness for remaining guilt and give to him the tenderness he built.	Save him, do not let him be consumed by flaming sword's fire. Let him arrive into Eden, with no memory of iniquity.	Holy Merciful One on High, observe the purity of his soul.

Fire, like G'vurah, sets a boundary.

TIFERET, MAJESTY, BALANCE - Hakafah 3			
Acronym and Attribute	Chorus	Behest	Availing Name of 42
נג"ד יכ"ש **תִּפְאֶרֶת**	וְיִשְׁלַח כַּפָּרָה לְאַשְׁמָתוֹ וְיִתֵּן אֵלָיו רַחֲמָיו:	וְיִזְכֶּה לִכְנֵס לְנוֹגַהּ וְעָנָן מְסֻכָּתוֹ וּבוֹ יַעֲלֶה וְלֹא יֵרֵד וְלֹא יִזָּכֵר לוֹ עָוֹן וָמֶרֶד	נָא גָדוֹל דָגוּל יְגַדֵּל כֹּחַ שְׁמִירָתוֹ
TIFERET	*V'yishlaḥ Kaparah L'Ashmato, V'yiten Eilav Raḥamav*	*V'yizkeh lica-neis l'nogah v'anan m'sukatoh, oovo ya-aleh v'lo yeireid, v'lo yizakheir lo avon va-mered*	***N**a **G**adol **D**agool **Y**'gadeil **K**o'ah **Sh**'mira-to*
Compassion Harmony Balance Maternal Mercy	Send forgiveness for remaining guilt and give to him the tenderness he built.	He will merit entry into Divine radiance, protected by cloud cover; in it he will ascend, and never fall, with iniquity or offense not recalled.	Please, Great Exalted (One), amplify the power of his protectors.

Tiferet is harmonious in nature and able to balance opposing forces.

NETZAH, ETERNITY, VICTORY - Hakafah 4			
Acronym and Attribute	Chorus	Behest	Availing Name of 42
בט"ר צת"ג נֵצַח	וְיִשְׁלַח כַּפָּרָה לַאֲשְׁמָתוֹ וְיִתֵּן אֵלָיו רַחֲמָיו׃	וּמִנַּחַל עֲדָנֶךָ תַּשְׁקֵהוּ וְיִפְתְּחוּ לוֹ שַׁעֲרֵי יְרוּשָׁלַיִם וּמִיכָאֵל יַקְרִיבֵהוּ לִפְנֵי שׁוֹכֵן שָׁמַיִם	בְּרַחֲמֵי טָהוֹר רַחֲמֵהוּ צְדָקָה תָּמִיד גָּמְלֵהוּ
NETZAḤ	*V'yishlaḥ Kaparah L'Ashmato, V'yiten Eilav Raḥamav*	*Oominaḥal adanekha tash'keihu v'yift'ḥu lo sha-arei Y'rushalyim, ooMikha-el yak'riveihu lifnei Shokhen Shamayim*	***B**'raḥamei **T**ahor **R**aḥameihu **Tz**'dakah, **T**amid, **G**am'leihu*
Sustain Focus Eternal Victory	Send forgiveness for remaining guilt and give to him the tenderness he built.	Through the channel of Your Eden, quench and satisfy him. Open the gates of *Yerushalayim* for him; Mikha'el will bring him close to the "*Shokhen Shamayim*," the One who dwells in the Heavens.	With pure compassion, be tender with him. See his merit, perpetually.

Netzah perseveres to victory

HOD, GRATITUDE, PAUSE – Hakafah 5			
Acronym and Attribute	Chorus	Behest	Availing Name of 42
חזק״ב טנ״ע הוד	וְיִשְׁלַח כַּפָּרָה לְאַשְׁמָתוֹ וְיִתֵּן אֵלָיו רַחֲמָיו׃	וּבֵית מִקְדָּשׁ וְאַפִּרְיוֹן יִפָּתְחוּ לוֹ בְּרָצוֹן וּמִכָאֵל יַכְנִיסֵהוּ בְּשָׂשׂוֹן בְּשִׂמְחָה וּבְשָׂשׂוֹן	חַי קָדוֹשׁ בָּרוּךְ טְהֵר נַפְשׁוֹ עֶלְיוֹן
HOD	*V'yishlaḥ Kaparah L'Ashmato, V'yiten Eilav Raḥamav*	*Ooveit Mik'dash, v'Apiryon, Yifat'ḥu Lo B'ratzon, ooMikha-el, Yakh'niseihau B'Sason, B'Simḥah oov'Sason.*	***Ḥ**ai **K**adosh, **B**arukh, **T**'heir, **N**af'sho **E**lyon*
Gratitude, Waits for impetus, Adaptive, Way of the Prophetess & Priestess	Send forgiveness for remaining guilt and give to him the tenderness he built.	The Temple and High Heavens will burst open with deep desire. Mikha'el will escort him in - with glee, with joy, with glee.	Living, holy, and Blessed One, purify his heavenly soul.

Hod knows which waves are clear for a good ride and which ones to let move on by.

YESOD, FOUNDATION, INTIMACY - Hakafah 6

Acronym and Attribute	Chorus	Behest	Availing Name of 42
יג"ל פז"ק יסוד	וְיִשְׁלַח כַּפָּרָה לְאַשְׁמָתוֹ וְיִתֵּן אֵלָיו רַחֲמָיו:	וְעַל מִזְבַּח הַקָּדוֹשׁ נִשְׁמָתוֹ תִהְיֶה נִצֶּבֶת וּמִפִּי עֶלְיוֹן שָׁם תִהְיֶה מְבוֹרֶכֶת	יָה גַלֵּה לַבֵּן פְּדוּתֶךָ זָךְ קָדוֹשׁ
YESOD	*V'yishlaḥ Kaparah L'Ashmato, V'yiten Eilav Raḥamav*	*V'al mizbaḥ hakadosh nishmato tih'yeh nitzevet,* *oomi-pi elyon sham tih'yeh m'vorekhet*	***YAH G**alei **L**aben **P**'dootekha, **Z**akh **K**adosh*
Foundation Intimacy	Send forgiveness for remaining guilt and give to him the tenderness he built.	On the holy altar, his *neshamah* will stand, and from Heavenly Mouth, there, he will be blessed.	**YAH**, reveal to Your redeemed son holy clarity.

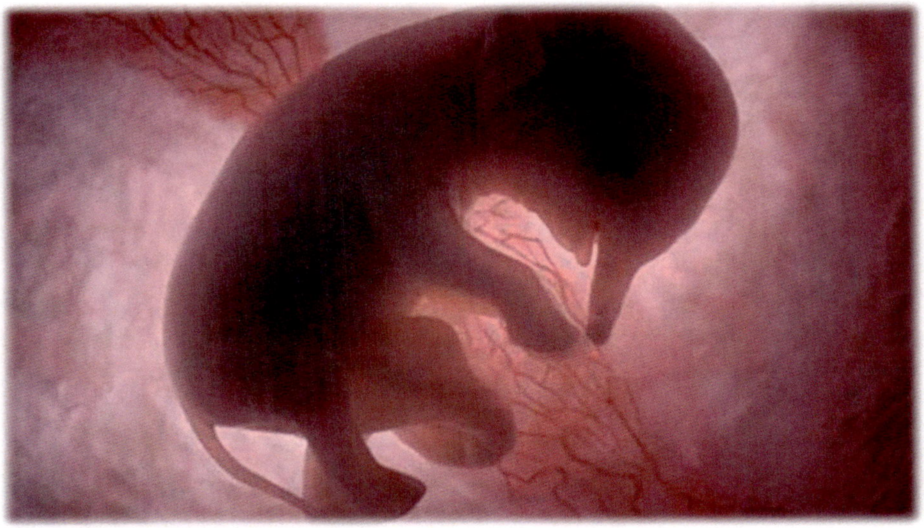

Yesod resonates intimacy, sexuality and fertility. The elephant in gestation, floating and being nourished in the womb, highlights the deep beauty of this most organic process.

SH'KHINAH, PRESENCE – Hakafah 7

Acronym and Attribute	Chorus	Behest	Availing Name of 42
שק״ו צי״ת מלכות	וְיִשְׁלַח כַּפָּרָה לְנִשְׁמָתוֹ וְיִתֵּן אֵלָיו רַחֲמָיו:	יִהְיֶה לְנֶפֶשׁ זֶה מַחֲזִיק וְתוֹמֵךְ וּבַעֲרָבוֹת לְפָנֶךָ יְשַׁמֵּשׁ יוֹמָם וָלַיְלָה לֹא יָמוּשׁ	שׁוֹכֵן קֶדֶם וּמֵאָז צֶדֶק יוֹשֶׁר תּוֹמֶךְ
SH'KHINAH [MALKHUT]	*V'yishlaḥ Caparah L'Nishmato, V'yiten Eilav Raḥamav*	*Yih'yeh l'nefesh zeh maḥazik v'tomeikh oova-aravot l'fanekha y'shameish v'yomam v'liyla lo yamush*	***Sh**okhen **K**edem **Oo**mei-az,* ***T**zedek **Y**osher **T**oomekha*
Majesty	Send forgiveness for remaining guilt and give to him the tenderness he built.	There will be strengthening and purity for this *nefesh*. And in the heavens, he will use them day and night, never ceasing.	Primordial Dweller, from earliest times till now, direct the virtuous integrity of Your purity.

Sh'khinah is Sovereign.

image by Barbara Mendes.

Through Time and Space your Glory Shines, Majestic One.	*Barookh shem k'vod malkhuto l'olam va'ed*	בָּרוּךְ שֵׁם כְּבוֹד מַלְכוּתוֹ לְעוֹלָם וָעֶד:

After the *hakafot,* chant the following verse:

And to the children of Avraham's concubines, Avraham gave gifts.[15]	*v'livnei hafilagshim asher* *l'Avraham* *natan Avraham matanot*	וְלִבְנֵ֤י הַפִּֽילַגְשִׁים֙ אֲשֶׁ֣ר לְאַבְרָהָ֔ם נָתַ֥ן אַבְרָהָ֖ם מַתָּנֹ֑ת

It is good to do this at the cemetery after saying *tzidduk hadin,* or at the home of the *meit* before lifting him up and carrying him (to his final resting place). [16]

[15] The Torah's concern for a concubine who had a child with Avraham reminds us of the need for inclusivity; to care for all mourners with comfort and kindness, especially where family matters get blurry or for relatives who are not part of the "inner" circle or are not Jewish.

[16] *Maavar Yabbok* Vilna Version 106 נד : *Ahavat Shalom* Version קכו

Probing the Mystery

Moshe Cordevero (1522-1570), a leader of the *Tz'fat* circle of Kabbalists, writes in his classic *Pardes Rimonim* 22:13, about the *Ana B'khoah*. Engaging with it activates the Divine Name of 42 hidden within, and invokes the initial condition of creation, the most potent light of Eden. Cordevero illustrates in great detail how the first 42 letters of *Breisheet* (Genesis) are encoded in the Name of 42. Each line of the *Ana B'khoah* resonates with a corresponding attribute of each of the Seven Lower *S'firot* on the *Etz Ḥayyim*.

The macrocosm of the *Etz Ḥayyim*, (the Tree of Life), models movement of the *Ohr Ein Sof* (The Light of The Infinite) into Earth's space-time continuum. The *Etz Ḥayyim* also models the Divine microcosm, the individual human. Being created in the Divine Image means human beings are a fractal, a microcosm, of this great Macrocosm. All of creation, angels, and the heavenly hosts have a place on this cosmic map. The upper three *S'firot* relate to movement of Divine Light and reflect into humans as consciousness and creativity. The lower seven *S'firot* relate to human emotion and action.

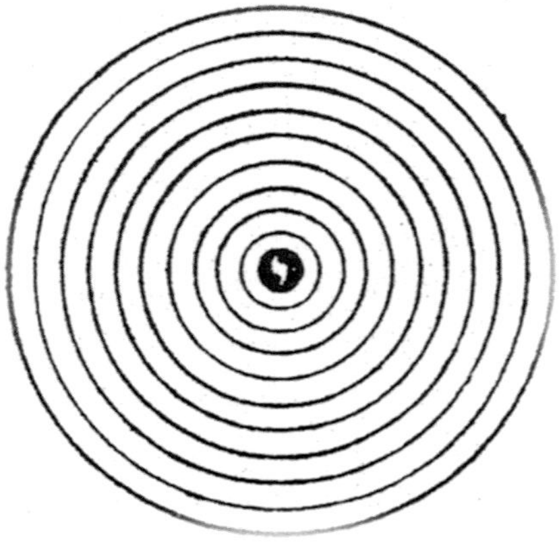

Feminine Tree of Life

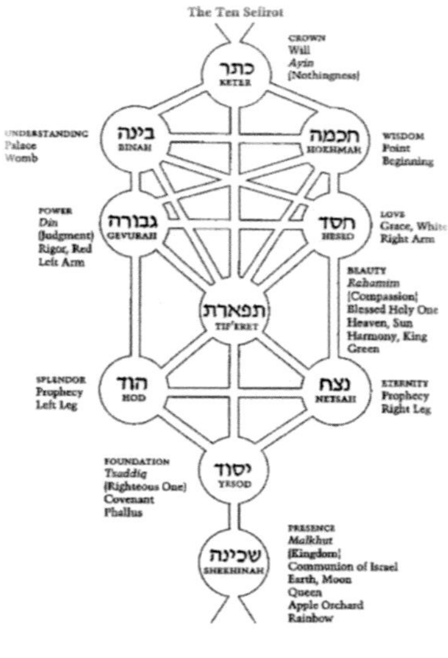

Masculine Tree of Life

On the previous page are two models of the Tree of Life - the one on the left is feminine and the one on the rights is masculine. We learn from the Holy Ari's Kabbalah in *Sefer Otzrot Ḥayyim HaMevuar*, an edited version of the *Etz Ḥayyim*, that they are both always true and operate simultaneously.

Images of DNA are represented below. There are two models: the double helix model (on the right) and a circuitous model representing a cross section of the vertical model above. DNA is a deep aspect of the substructure of life and movement. While there are similarities within species, DNA is unique to an individual. These images are accessed through the brilliance of contemporary science.

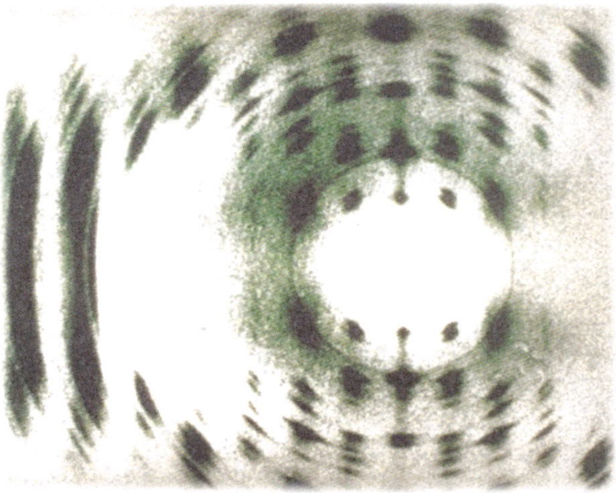

Cross-section of DNA resembles feminine Tree of Life

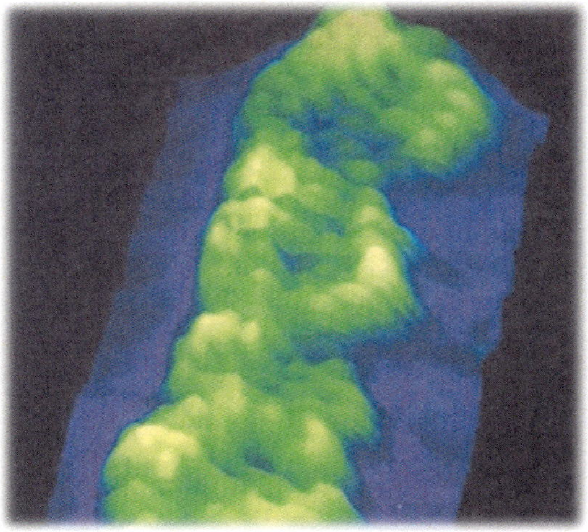

Double-helix model of DNA resembles masculine Tree of Life

Seven Lower S'firot Associations

In this chart, by Rabbi Zalman Schachter-Shalomi *zt"l,* the movement of the seven lower *S'firot* is described by archetypical associations and as a continuum of virtue to vice. The matriarchs are from Meta Parshiyot by Rabbi David Wolfe-Blank *zt"l.*

DIVINE S'FIRAH	*ARCHETYPE FEMALE*	*ARCHETYPE MALE*	*VIRTUE*	*VICE*
HESED *(Grace)*	Miryam	Avraham	Love	Lust/Obsession
GEVURAH *(Severity)*	Leah	Yitzhak	Respect	Fear/Terror
TIFERET *(Beauty)*	Ḥannah	Yisrael (Yaakov)	Compassion/Balance	Indulgence
NETZAḤ *(Victory)*	Rivkah	Moshe	Efficiency	Pedantry
HOD *(Glory)*	Sarah	Aharon	Humility Esthetics	Self-Denigration Vanity
YESOD *(Foundation)*	Tamar	Yoseph	Vulnerability/Intimacy	Promiscuity
SH'KHINAH [MALKHUT] *(Majesty)*	Raḥel	David	Surrender/Receptivity	Stubbornness

שקו צית	יגל פזק	חקב טנע	בטר צתג	נגד יכש	קרע שטן	אבג יתץ
שביעי	ששי	חמישי	רביעי	שלישי	שני	ראשון
פה	נחיר שמאל	נחיר ימין	אזן שמאל	אזן ימין	עין שמאל	עין ימין
ממשלה	זרע	עושר	חן	שלום	חכמה	חיים

Sefer Yetzirah, 4:11, excerpt from a commentary attributed to the RAvaD (Rabbi Avraham ben David).

Cycle	1	2	3	4	5	6	7
S'firah	***Ḥesed***	***G'vurah***	***Tiferet***	***Netzaḥ***	***Hod***	***Yesod***	***Sh'khinah***
Attribute	Benevolence	Power Discipline Boundary	Truth Balance	Tenacity	Gratitude	Foundation	Presence
Head	Right Eye	Left Eye	Right Ear	Left Ear	Right Nostril	Left Nostril	Mouth
Orienta-tion	Life	Wisdom	Peace	Charm (Coherence)	Wealth	Seed	Authority

Translation by Rabbi Zalman Schachter-Shalomi (*zt"l*)

חֶסֶד

ḤESED; Lovingkindness

אֵל

(אב"ג ית"ץ)

Day 1

Water

Expansion

Fill out; expand to limits

Meets any container

Avraham, Miryam

Right Arm

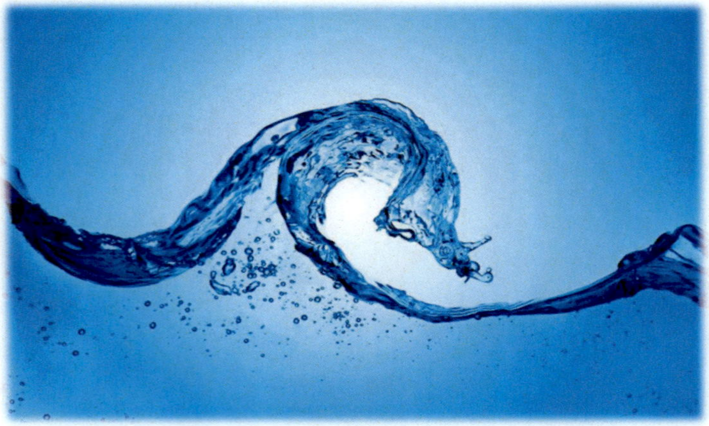

Hesed...

גְבוּרָה

G'VURAH; Boundary

אלהים

(קר"ע שט"ן)

Day 2

Fire

Contraction

Control and adjust

Membrane—channel for giving

Yitzhak, Leah

Left Arm

G'vurah…

תִּפְאֶרֶת

TIFERET; Beauty

יהוה

(נג"ד יכ"ש)

Day 3

Air

Balance, harmony

Blend and harmonize

Maternal compassion in giving and receiving

Yaakov, Hannah

Torso

Tiferet...

נֶצַח

NETZAH; Eternity, Victory

יהוה צְבָאוֹת

(בט"ר צת"ג)

Day 4

Perseverance

Design a prototype

Staying the course

Moshe, Rivkah

Right Leg

Netzah...

הוֹד

HOD; Gratitude, Waiting

אֱלֹהִים צְבָאוֹת

(חזק"ב טנ"ע)

Day 5

Grace, gratitude

Refine

Waiting for an impetus, discerning if it for you to act on

Aharon, Sarah

Left Leg

Hod...

יְסוֹד

YESOD; Foundation

אֵל חַי, אֵל שַׁדַּי

(יג״ל פז״ק)

Day 6

Sexuality, bonding

Duplicate

Being intimate and vulnerable

Yosef, Tamar

Pelvis

Yesod...

שְׁכִינָה [מַלְכוּת]

SH'KHINAH [MALKHUT]; Sovereignty

אֲדֹנָי

(שק"ו צי"ת)

Day 7

Receiving, grounding

Birth

Receiving Presence, experiencing completion

David, Rahel

Skin/Feet—the part of us that interfaces with Earth

Sh'khinah...

About the Author

Rabbi T'mimah Audrey Ickovits, BSE, is a teacher, scholar, and ritual artist.

Devoted to the environment and committed to equality in death Rabbi T'mimah teaches about Jewish Green Burial. Passionate about ancestral wisdom and bringing it forward to inform contemporary challenges, Rabbi T'mimah compiles siddurim making traditional liturgy, devotional translations and songs, and kabbalah practices easily accessible in English. As the spiritual leader of Holistic Jew, she is dedicated to cultivating new and old methods of cultivating the Divine feminine. Rabbi T'mimah teaches Continuum Movement Liquid Kabbalah integrating Kabbalah wisdom into sacred movement.

You can learn more about her work at www.HolisticJew.org.

Rabbi T'mimah Audrey Ickovits
www.HolisticJew.org
https://www.facebook.com/HolisticJew/

Made in the USA
Middletown, DE
17 July 2024

57490252R00033